A
gift
honoring
Griffin
and
Carson
Gilchrist

Catastrophic Colorado!

The History and Science of Our Natural Disasters

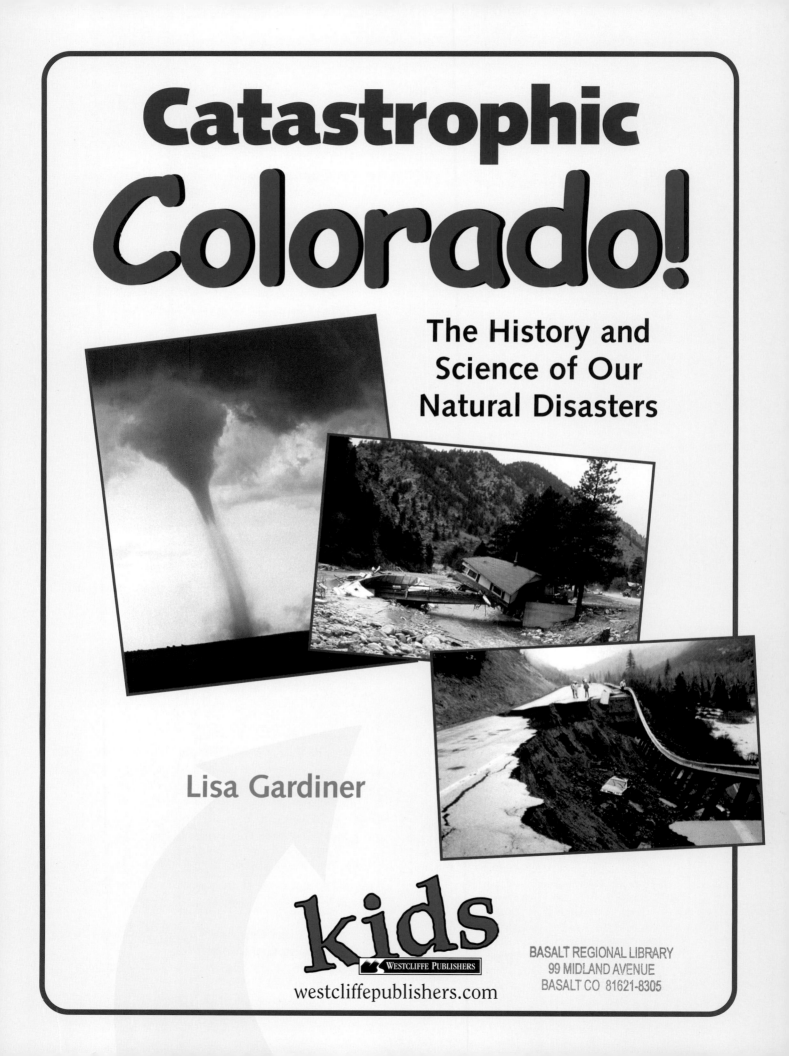

Lisa Gardiner

kids

WESTCLIFFE PUBLISHERS

westcliffepublishers.com

International Standard Book Numbers
ISBN-10: 1-56579-549-0
ISBN-13: 978-1-56579-549-5

Text and illustrations copyright: Lisa Gardiner, 2006.
All rights reserved.
Photography copyright: As credited with photographs.
All rights reserved.
Editor: Jennifer Jahner
Designer: Kimberlee Lynch
Production Manager: Craig Keyzer

Published by:
Westcliffe Publishers, Inc.
P.O. Box 1261
Englewood, CO 80150

Printed in China by Hing Yip Printing Co. Ltd.

Library of Congress Cataloging-in-Publication Data:
Gardiner, Lisa, 1973-
  Catastrophic Colorado! : the history and science of
our natural disasters / Lisa Gardiner.
      p. cm.

  ISBN-13: 978-1-56579-549-5
  ISBN-10: 1-56579-549-0
  1. Natural disasters--Colorado--Juvenile literature.
I. Title.
  GB5010.G37 2006
  363.3409788--dc22
                                    2006015240

*For more information about other fine books and
calendars from Westcliffe Publishers, please contact
your local bookstore, call us at 1-800-523-3692, or
visit us on the Web at* **westcliffepublishers.com**.

Cover Photos: *Left:* Avalanche at Red Mountain Pass,
Colorado, February 28, 1987.
Right: A cloud-to-ground lightning strike.

The author and publisher of this book have made every
effort to ensure the accuracy and currency of its
information. Nevertheless, books can require revisions.
Please feel free to let us know if you find information
in this book that needs to be updated, and we will be
glad to correct it for the next printing. Your comments
and suggestions are always welcome.

Photo Credits

Acknowledgments
• **Page 4:** Photo courtesy of the United States Geological Survey

About This Book
• **Page 5:** Photo courtesy of the United States Geological Survey

Crash! Boom! Thunderstorms, Lightning, and Hail
• **Cover & page 6:** Photo courtesy of the National Oceanic & Atmospheric Administration
• **Pages 9 & 10 (right):** Photos courtesy of Carlye Calvin
• **Page 10 (left):** Photo courtesy of Lisa Gardiner

Twisters Are Tornadoes
• **Pages 12 & 17:** Photos courtesy of Verne Carlson
• **Pages 1 & 15:** Photo © University Corporation for Atmospheric Research Digital Image Library
• **Page 16:** Photo courtesy of Carlye Calvin

Climb to Safety! Flash Floods
• **Pages 1, 18, 19, & 21:** Photos courtesy of the United States Geological Survey
• **Page 20:** Photos courtesy of Anne Pharamond

Blown Away! Windy Weather
• **Page 23:** Photo courtesy of Lisa Gardiner

Watch for Wildfires!
• **Page 25 & 27:** Photos courtesy of the National Park Service
• **Page 26:** Photo courtesy of the National Aeronautics and Space Administration

Snow Day! Blizzards and Snowstorms
• **Page 30:** Photo courtesy of Carlye Calvin
• **Pages 31, 33, 34, & 35:** Photos courtesy of Anne Pharamond

Awesome Avalanches
• **Page 36 (left):** Photos by Tim Lane, courtesy of the Colorado Geological Survey and Colorado Avalanche Information Center
• **Cover & page 36 (right):** Photo by Dale Atkins, courtesy of the Colorado Geological Survey and Colorado Avalanche Information Center
• **Page 38:** Photos courtesy of the United States Geological Survey

Earthquakes in Colorado?
• **Page 41:** Photo courtesy of Lisa Gardiner

The Mountains Are Falling Down! Rockfalls and Landslides
• **Pages 1, 44, & 45:** Photos courtesy of the United States Geological Survey

Contents

Acknowledgments

I'm very grateful to Brenda Porter at the Colorado Mountain Club, who sparked my interest in the science of Colorado's awesome natural events, Gretchen Hanisch, who helped me channel this interest into the initial idea for this book, and Anne Pharamond, who read the book along the way and offered helpful suggestions and encouragement.

Thanks to many folks who offered advice, support, and some pretty impressive photographs, including Vince Mathews and the Colorado Geological Survey, Carlye Calvin, Verne Carlson, and the team at UCAR Education and Outreach.

—Lisa Gardiner

Avalanche-damaged buildings of the Liberty Bell Mine

About This Book

If you have picked out this book, then you are probably interested in the catastrophic things that can happen in Colorado. The word *catastrophe* means disaster. Colorado is a beautiful place, with tall mountains, broad plains, long rivers, and deep canyons. But it also has all sorts of natural events that we call catastrophes when they cause harm to people or to the places where people live. Natural events like these are not considered catastrophes or disasters when they cause no harm to people or homes. Sometimes natural events are very small and cause little damage. Sometimes they are huge. All of the events described in this book are natural events, but some—like flash floods, wildfires, avalanches, earthquakes, and landslides—can also be caused by people.

Like most scary things, these events make us curious. The real nice thing about books, though, is that flipping the pages will not put you in harm's way. This book lets you learn about the sorts of catastrophic events that can happen and have happened in Colorado, as well as the science behind them. And understanding how they happen is the first step to staying safe! *Happy reading!*

The sand dunes in Great Sand Dunes National Park and Preserve are created and moved by the wind.

Sometimes puffy, sheep-shaped clouds in the sky grow into large, dark clouds in just a few hours. When you see large and dark clouds, especially in the spring and summer, there is a good chance that a thunderstorm will happen soon. A thunderstorm usually includes thunder, lightning, and rain. Often, a thunderstorm will also include hail and sometimes even tornadoes. Thunderstorms are common during spring in Colorado because the air up high is cold, while the air near the ground is beginning to warm. The cold air and warm air move around. Warm air rises higher and cold air sinks toward the ground. The shifting air can lead to noisy thunderstorms. Read on to learn how this works.

A cloud-to-ground lightning strike

How Do Thunderstorms Happen?

There are several different ways that thunderstorms form. This is one way that they form in Colorado. First, heat from the sun warms the ground all day long. The air near the ground is warmed and it rises. As it rises, the air spreads out and cools down. Cool air can't hold as much water vapor (evaporated water) in it as warm air. The vapor comes out of the air, making the tiny droplets that form

10:00 AM 12:00 PM 2:00 PM

clouds. All afternoon this happens over and over again. Warm air rises and then cools, and this adds more tiny droplets of water to the cloud. The growing cloud can become a thunderstorm!

How Lightning and Thunder Are Formed

Inside a thunderstorm cloud, tiny, invisible particles called molecules are moving around and pushing past

each other. When molecules bump against each other, little pieces called electrons are rubbed off. Electrons are negatively charged. Positively charged particles on the ground are attracted to them just like a magnet is attracted to the refrigerator. The positive charges will move up tall objects so that they are closer to the negatively charged part of a storm cloud. They cannot travel up just any object, however. They can only travel through

materials that are called *conductors*, such as trees, metal flagpoles, and objects made mostly of water, like people.

Eventually, the negative particles in the cloud and the positive particles on the ground move to meet each other. When they meet, the energy heats the air, causing a flash of light. That's lightning! Lightning can also happen within a cloud, or from one cloud to another.

The boom of thunder happens at the same time as the lightning. As the lightning flashes, the air molecules spread apart and then shrink back together very quickly. This makes the thunder noise. If you are very close to where lightning strikes, you will see the flash of light and hear the boom of noise at the same time. If you are far away from the lightning strike, you will see the flash of light before you hear the boom of thunder because light travels faster than sound.

Colorado Thunderstorm Facts

- Most of Colorado's mountain areas and much of the High Plains have thunderstorms 50–100 days of the year. Some of these storms only last a few minutes.

- There are only 20–50 thunderstorm days each year in western Colorado.

- Most thunderstorms happen in spring and summer.

- Lightning is the most dangerous weather hazard in Colorado, according to the National Weather Service.

- Of all the 50 states, Colorado has the 11th-highest number of lightning strikes on people.

A thunderstorm near Limon, Colorado

How Hail Forms

Hail is a shower of stones made of ice that falls during some thunderstorms. A hailstone can be small like a pea or as large as a grapefruit. Hailstones, even small ones, can cause damage to car windshields, roofs, and plants. Large hailstones are fascinating but they can also be unpleasant. No one wants to be hit on the head with a grapefruit-size ball of ice!

Not all thunderstorms make hail. For hail to form, there must be very cold air at the tops of storm clouds. Water freezes in the cold air, making ice. The ice is kept high in the air by winds. It bounces around in the storm cloud and grows larger as more water droplets freeze onto it. Eventually the hailstones become too heavy to be held up by the wind, or the wind stops blowing, and they fall to the ground.

Colorado has much more hail than in other places where thunderstorms happen. This is because the land in Colorado is higher up than other places. Most places in Colorado are a mile or more above the level of the oceans. This makes Colorado closer to the cold layers of air where hail forms, so it is less likely that the hail will have time to melt as it falls to the ground.

Right: Golf-ball–size hailstones.
Left: Small hailstones fall during an afternoon thunderstorm in Denver, Colorado.

Severe Thunderstorm Watch

This means that a thunderstorm is likely to form. If there is a Severe Thunderstorm Watch, stay informed about the weather and watch the sky for changes. Get inside if you see lightning.

Severe Thunderstorm Warning

This warning means that a meteorologist (a weather scientist) has spotted a thunderstorm either using his or her eyes or using a radar tool that detects precipitation and winds. If a Severe Thunderstorm Warning is issued, it is time to get inside to stay safe!

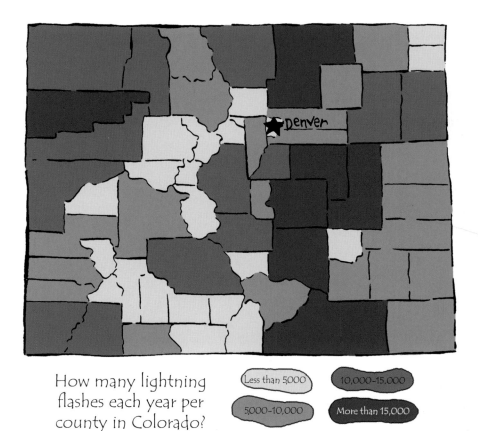

How many lightning flashes each year per county in Colorado?

Less than 5,000   10,000-15,000

5,000-10,000   More than 15,000

Twisters Are Tornadoes

Tornadoes, sometimes called twisters, are small but fierce storms. Tornadoes happen as part of large thunderstorms. Their spiraling winds move at high speeds and are very dangerous. When the spiraling winds "touch down" to the ground, houses, barns, crops, cars, and anything else that's in the path of the storm is damaged or destroyed. The world's strongest tornadoes, with winds up to 300 miles per hour, happen more often in our neighbor states like Kansas. Most tornadoes in Colorado are smaller, though they can still cause damage to homes, trees, cars, and sometimes people.

This small tornado touched down in Boulder, Colorado, in 1997. Loud tornado sirens blared, warning people that a tornado was spotted.

Where Do Tornadoes Occur in Colorado?

Tornadoes have been reported from all over the state, but they are very uncommon in central and western Colorado. The largest numbers of tornadoes are spotted east of the Rocky Mountains. This eastern part of Colorado is on the edge of "tornado alley," the area including much of the central United States where most of the large thunderstorms that produce tornadoes form. In this area, cold and dry air from Canada travels south and meets warm, moist air traveling north from the Gulf of Mexico. When the

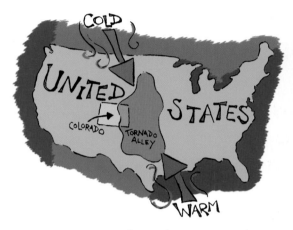

cold air and the warm air meet, giant thunderstorms form, causing lightning and rain, and sometimes flooding, hail, and tornadoes. A tornado will form if air begins to rotate when it comes in contact with winds moving at different speeds. Warm air rises and causes the rotating air to speed up, creating a cloud shaped like a funnel.

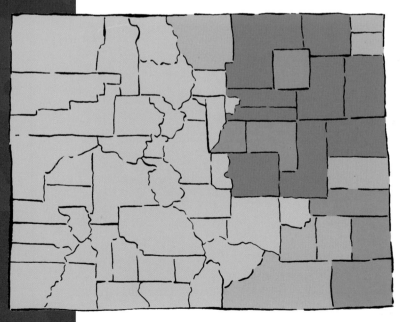

Between 1950 and 2003, 1,563 tornadoes happened in Colorado. This map of the state shows which counties had the most.

0–20 tornadoes

20–40 tornadoes

40–60 tornadoes

more than 60 tornadoes

When Do They Happen in Colorado?

Tornadoes happen typically in the spring and summer in Colorado. Most occur in June. However, tornadoes have been spotted in Colorado during nine months of the year. Tornadoes are most common in the afternoon and early evening, but they can form at all times of day. About 9 out of 10 of Colorado's tornadoes develop between 1 p.m. and 9 p.m.

Tornadoes Are Not All the Same!

Weak tornadoes: Nearly 9 out of 10 tornadoes in our state last less than 10 minutes and have wind speeds of less than 110 miles per hour (mph). That is weak for a tornado! But winds this strong can cause damage to wooden buildings and mobile homes, and can break windows and tree branches.

Strong tornadoes: About 1 out of 10 tornadoes in Colorado is considered strong. Strong tornadoes may last more than 20 minutes and can travel as far as 25 miles. Strong tornadoes have wind speeds up to 200 mph, which can blow roofs off buildings, destroy mobile homes, knock trees down, and flip cars over.

Violent tornadoes: Only about 1 out of every 100 tornadoes in Colorado is considered violent. These super strong tornadoes are pretty uncommon, but they are able to completely destroy homes and other buildings.

Colorado Tornado Facts

- 600 tornadoes were spotted in Colorado in 10 years (1995–2005).

- 1998 was a record year, with 98 tornadoes—about twice the usual amount.

- On June 15, 1988, five tornadoes moved across Denver, causing millions of dollars in damage. Luckily, no one was killed.

- The world's largest tornadoes can cause massive destruction in an area that is 1 mile wide by 50 miles long! No tornadoes that large have ever been seen in Colorado.

A tornado in southeast Colorado

Tornado Watches and Warnings

Are tornadoes likely to be found in your area this afternoon? The National Weather Service warns people when tornadoes are likely, or when one has been spotted. Local television and radio stations spread the news.

 Tornado Watch: This means that weather conditions make it likely that tornadoes will develop. Keep your eye on the sky and be prepared to head inside.

! Tornado Warning: This means that a meteorologist or a weather instrument has spotted a tornado. If a Tornado Warning is issued for your area, go inside a sturdy building. Go to the basement if there is one, or to an interior room, hallway, or closet.

 Do you hear sirens? Some cities in Colorado have noisy sirens to warn people of tornadoes. If you hear the sirens blast, head inside and take cover.

A mini tornado, called a "gustnado," travels over the plains.

Tornado Safety

Where can you avoid a tornado? Underground!
Tornadoes can't go there! If it is possible, head to the basement of a sturdy building or into an underground storm shelter if you are near one. Mobile homes are not safe places to stay during tornado weather. If the building you are in doesn't have a basement, go to a room, closet, or hallway in the middle of the house on the lowest floor. Stay far from windows! Cover up with blankets or get under a table to protect yourself from flying objects.

If you are in a car and see a tornado, the driver should drive away from it. But if the tornado is moving quickly, it can catch up to your car. In this case, get out of the car. If there are no sturdy buildings nearby to take shelter within, lie facedown in a dry ditch away from the car and cover your head.

This tornado happened in 2004 on the plains in Elbert County, Colorado.

This safety information is based on recommendations by the National Weather Service.

Flash Floods

>>>>>

A flash flood can happen with little or no warning. In Colorado, flash floods have happened when dams broke or because of heavy thunderstorms. During a flash flood, large amounts of water flow through narrow valleys, changing a peaceful stream into a violent flood within minutes. The change is so fast that the water can arrive as a large wall, up to 30 feet high, roaring down the valley. The fast-moving waters of a flash flood are so powerful that they can roll boulders and destroy buildings, bridges, cars, and trees. Flash floods are rare and very dangerous events.

The flood of the Big Thompson River was powerful enough to move houses. This house was left on top of a bridge once the floodwaters were gone.

Flash Floods Made by Rain

Most flash floods in Colorado are natural events caused when many inches of rain fall in a short amount of time. The longer the rainstorm lasts, the more likely it is that there will be a flash flood. Slow-moving thunderstorms are especially dangerous because all of the heavy rains fall in one place, which makes a flood more likely.

The shape of the land is also very important. In valleys with steep sides, water does not have any space to spread out and slow down, so it keeps moving downhill quickly. Valleys that are very wide and flat can flood when there is too much water, but the water will be able to spread out, stay shallower, and move more slowly. Listen for distant thunder when you are visiting a steep-sided river valley. It is possible for a thunderstorm that is miles upstream to cause flooding where you are standing.

Sometimes some of the water seeps underground instead of flowing over the surface. The water seeps into the spaces between pebbles and grains of sand in the ground. However, in many areas of Colorado, the ground is made of solid rock or the soil is hard with few spaces in it. The rainwater does not soak in easily and runs off.

Big Thompson Flash Flood

Saturday, July 31, 1976, was a beautiful day and many people were out enjoying Colorado's mountains and valleys, including the canyon of the Big Thompson River. A thunderstorm formed that afternoon high in the mountains. Unlike most Colorado thunderstorms, it did not move much. The thunderstorm stayed put, dumping oodles of rain (10–12 inches of it). The rainwater collected, forming a wall of water 19 feet high. The wall

The Big Thompson Flash Flood moved tons of sand. Once the floodwaters were gone, this truck was left trapped in sand.

of water then roared down the canyon of the Big Thompson River. The people who were there said that it made as much noise as jet engines. As it pushed down the canyon, the flood moved 300,000 cubic yards of debris, including torn-apart buildings and 197 cars. More than a hundred people were killed in the flood and millions of dollars in property was damaged.

Lawn Lake Flash Flood

In 1903, a group of farmers built a dam to triple the size of Lawn Lake, high in the Rocky Mountains. They used the water from Lawn Lake for watering crops in the town of Loveland on the High Plains. There are no roads to Lawn Lake and it is a 6-mile hike to get to it. And so the dam was not taken care of as often as it should have been and had not been repaired for many years.

Early in the morning of July 15, 1982, the Lawn Lake dam broke. People camping along the Roaring River below the dam reported that a wall of water 25–30 feet high came down the valley. It was a sunny day so nobody expected a flood. The water picked up and carried sand and rocks of all sizes down the river. The water slowed down as it entered a wide valley and dropped many of the boulders, sand grains, and pebbles it carried in a fan shape at the valley's edge. This made a feature called an *alluvial fan*. The water continued to travel more slowly down the valley and eventually reached another dam, which broke as well, flooding the town of Estes Park.

Top: During the Lawn Lake Flood, boulders, pebbles, and sand were dumped into a pile.
Bottom: The pile of rocks dumped by the Lawn Lake Flood looks like a fan from above.

Flash Flood Safety

Along many narrow valleys that are more prone to flooding, there are signs that tell travelers to leave their cars and climb to safety if there is a flash flood. It only

The town of Estes Park, Colorado, flooded during the Lawn Lake Flood.

takes a foot or two of fast-moving water to sweep a car away. Flash flood waters move much faster than cars, so it is unlikely that you will be able to race a flash flood and win. Instead, leave the car and climb up the sides of the valley.

When visiting Colorado's valleys, stay safe by watching and listening for the warning signs. Listen for thunder either nearby or upstream. The rain from a thunderstorm could cause a flood. Watch the water level in the river or stream within the valley. If it is rising fast, look for a high place that you could get to safely.

If it looks like a flash flood might happen, or if there has been a flash flood, the radio and television news will broadcast warnings to let people know of the danger.

Flash Flood Watch

This means that conditions are right for a flash flood to happen. Be alert and prepared to leave the area.

Flash Flood Warning

This means that a flash flood is happening or is about to happen. If a flash flood warning is issued for the area where you are, get out of valleys and away from rivers immediately! Climb to safety!

Sometimes Colorado can be a very blustery place. Colorado's strong winds can blow trees over, blow roofs off buildings, and damage power lines. Sometimes Colorado's windy weather is part of a storm and other times it is not. Read on to discover why some of this windy weather happens.

Windy Blasts From Above

During a *downburst*, winds blast down from above. Colorado gets many small and powerful downbursts, called *microbursts*, that are a part of thunderstorms. When the blast reaches the ground, it blows across the land at speeds up to 150 mph (but usually less than 100 mph). Sometimes in Colorado, microbursts happen during a thunderstorm, but often they happen when skies are gloomy but rain is not falling. Microbursts happen in a pretty small area, usually less than 2 miles wide. So

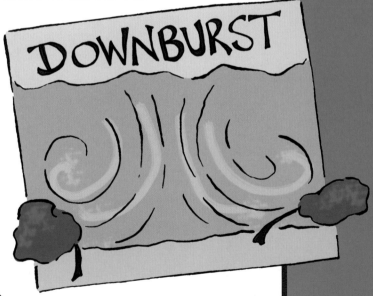

people on one side of town might have just experienced a regular thunderstorm or even just gloomy skies while people on the other side of town experienced the speedy winds of a microburst.

Warm Chinook Winds

Sometimes during winter in Colorado, wind traveling from west to east zooms down the eastern slope of the Rocky Mountains and flows over the High Plains. These winds happen often enough that they have been given a special name. They are called *Chinook winds*. Unlike other types of windy weather, when Chinook winds are blowing, temperatures east of the Rocky Mountains become warmer. The winds are warm compared with the usual winter temperatures and they can be very powerful. On January 1, 1963, Chinook winds sped through Denver at speeds of more than 80 mph, causing damage to buildings and power lines and warming up Denver and the High Plains to 70 degrees Fahrenheit.

Chinook is a Native American word that means "snow eater." Chinook winds don't really eat the snow, but they do get rid of it pretty quickly. The winds are very dry and are much warmer than snow. So if they start blowing down the mountains, any snow on the ground will melt into water or *sublimate*, meaning it will turn into vapor in the air.

Chinook winds happen during the winter, when the eastern side of the Rocky Mountains is not warmed as much by the sun. During other times of the year, the sun warms up the mountains much more. The air near the surface of the mountains warms and rises, pushing the winds up so they cannot zoom down the mountainsides.

These trees are growing high on a mountainside where winds are often very strong. They have few branches on the side where the wind usually comes from.

Wildfires are uncontrolled fires in natural places like grasslands and forests. Every year in Colorado there are about 2,500 wildfires. Some are large and others are small. Colorado wildfires are most likely to happen in the summer when there is less rain and more heat and lightning.

How Do Wildfires Get Started?

Many wildfires are started naturally, although careless people start some of them, too. There are three things that are needed for a fire to start. Fires need heat, oxygen from the air, and something to burn. The stuff that burns is usually dry wood, bushes, and grass, but some fires burn coal, found in the rocks near the ground's surface. Natural fires are usually started by heat from the sun or by lightning strikes. People accidentally start fires with out-of-control campfires, cigarettes, matches, and fireworks. Colorado's dry climate means that it is not always safe to have a campfire.

WHAT HELPS A WILDFIRE TO BURN?

HEAT FROM THE SUN

LIGHTNING

OXYGEN-IN-THE AIR

WIND

FUEL

Some wildfires only burn a few acres of land, while others spread to huge areas. The amount that a wildfire spreads depends on the amount of stuff that is available to burn. That stuff is called *fuel*. In forests, dead trees, bushes, and grasses are the fuel for the fire. On the High Plains, dried grasses and small shrubs are fuel. Small fuels such as grass and pinecones burn quickly. The amount that a fire can spread also depends on the weather. Dry weather and high temperatures cause a fire to continue to burn and spread. Winds provide oxygen to the flames and help fires spread over the land. On the other hand, a rainstorm can help slow a fire. Where a fire is able to spread also depends on the shape of the land. Fires can travel up hills faster than they travel down.

Fires: Good or Bad?

Uncontrolled fires of any type are dangerous to people, houses, and animals. Fires cause other hazards, too. After a

A forest fire in Rocky Mountain National Park in 1916 burned most of the trees in this area of the park. Today new trees have grown back, but there is still evidence of the fire.

fire has swept through, the area is more likely to have flooding and landslides.

So how can a dangerous wildfire also be good for the land? Small fires can clear out the dead wood from an area without killing the living trees. In fact, in many parks, controlled fires are set by park rangers to clear away dead

COLORADO

NEW MEXICO

The smoke from wildfires can be seen from space. This image taken from a satellite in the summer of 2002 shows smoke from the Hayman Fire and others burning in Colorado and New Mexico.

wood, making uncontrolled wildfires less likely to start. Many plant species thrive in fire-prone areas. For example, the cones of lodgepole pine trees are opened by fire. The seeds in the cones are dropped onto rich soil left by the fire and will grow into new trees.

The Hayman Fire

The catastrophic Hayman Fire, which burned southwest of Denver in 2002, was the largest wildfire in Colorado history. Despite the hundreds of firefighters battling the flames, the Hayman Fire burned for nearly a month, from

June 8 until July 2, 2002. The fire was started by a person burning an illegal campfire. At the time, no campfires were allowed in the forest because of very dry conditions. The campfire spread, eventually burning more than 135,000 acres (210 square miles) of forest. At least 5,000 people had to be evacuated from the area. The fire burned 133 homes and caused $40,000,000 in damage. There had not been as much snow as usual in Colorado's mountains during the winter before the fire, so there was less snow on mountains to melt, and less water flowing in Colorado's rivers during the spring. The dry conditions and windy weather helped the fire to spread.

After firefighters put out the Hayman Fire, the burned land was in danger of floods and mudslides, and dead trees were falling. A team of scientists, engineers, and other specialists designed a plan to help repair the waterways and ecosystems. Grass seed was planted to help keep the soil in place. Less than a year after the fire, wildflowers and small aspen trees began to grow in the burned area.

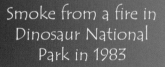
Smoke from a fire in Dinosaur National Park in 1983

Not only is Colorado far away from the oceans, it is high above the oceans, too! The height of the oceans is called *sea level*. The height of land above sea level is called *altitude*. The highest parts of Colorado are in the Rocky Mountains, where the tops of 54 mountains are more than 14,000 feet above sea level. However, even the flat places in Colorado are thousands of feet above sea level. Colorado has the highest altitudes of any place in the continental United States.

Why Is the Air Thin in Colorado?

At sea level, particles of air called *air molecules* are packed together closely. But in high-altitude places like Colorado, the air molecules are spread farther apart. This means that a breath of air at low altitude has more air molecules in it than a breath of air from a high Colorado mountaintop. Some people say that there is "thin air" at high altitudes because there are less air molecules in each breath.

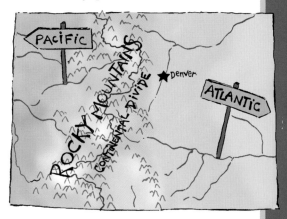

The highest altitudes in Colorado are found in the Rocky Mountains. To the east, all water flows toward the Atlantic Ocean. To the west, all water flows toward the Pacific.

Colorado's high altitude is not a catastrophic event. In fact, the thin air caused by high altitudes is in Colorado all the time. Sometimes, though, the "thin air" can make people sick. Read on to discover how this happens.

Altitude Sicknesses

We need to breathe air to survive. The part of the air that we need is the oxygen. But the higher the altitude, the less air there is in each breath, so the less oxygen gets into a person's body. People can become ill in Colorado's mountains because they are not getting enough oxygen. Most illnesses are very mild, but a few are serious.

Because of the altitude, some people who are used to living at sea level might feel a little sick when they first get to places like Denver (5,280 feet above sea level), Leadville (10,152 feet above sea level), or even higher. They might have a headache, an upset stomach, or trouble sleeping. People who are used to high altitudes might feel ill if they go up even higher. This mild altitude illness is called *acute mountain sickness*. Other types of altitude sickness can be very severe and are also very rare.

When you go to an altitude that is higher than you are used to, your body tries to adjust to having less air molecules. Your heart beats faster and you breathe more often. Most people who visit Colorado adjust to the altitude without any problems. Keep yourself healthy by not going up in altitude too quickly, getting extra rest, and drinking more water than you usually do as your body adjusts. Take it easy for a few days because your heart and lungs have to do more work when you are at high altitude. If you feel sick, go down to lower altitude.

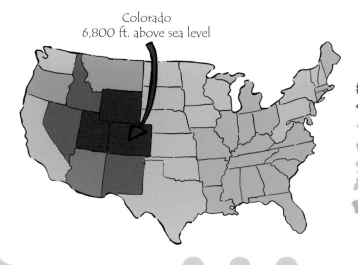

Colorado
6,800 ft. above sea level

Average elevation of states

- 6,000–7,000 ft.
- 5,000–6,000 ft.
- 4,000–5,000 ft.
- 3,000–4,000 ft.
- 2,000–3,000 ft.
- 1,000–2,000 ft.
- Less than 1,000 ft.

Blizzards and Snowstorms

Some winter storms bring heavy snow to Colorado's High Plains, while others dump several feet of white fluffy snow on Colorado's mountain slopes. A snowstorm is any storm during which snow falls. But once in a while a huge storm happens. These huge winter storms are called blizzards. They leave a thick blanket of snow behind. As the snow falls during a blizzard, it blows around in strong winds of more than 35 mph. This means that being in a blizzard is like being in a snow globe that has been shaken. The blowing snow makes it difficult to see even a few feet in front of you!

Nederland, Colorado, after the 2003 blizzard

How Do Big Snowstorms Happen?

For a big snowstorm to happen in Colorado, two things are needed: cold temperatures and a storm with lots of moisture. The moisture is what makes the snowflakes. Cold temperatures cause snow to fall instead of rain.

Many of the storms that bring snow to the mountains come from the west. These storms pick up lots of moisture from the Pacific Ocean and then travel eastward. As the moist air travels east, it is forced up to higher altitudes to cross over mountain ranges like Colorado's Rocky Mountains. When pushed up to higher altitudes, air can't hold as much moisture, so snow falls. By the time the storm gets to the eastern side of

This car in Denver was nearly covered with snow during the 2003 blizzard.

the Rocky Mountains, it has lost most of its moisture, so Denver and the High Plains don't get much snow from this type of storm.

A different type of storm brings big heaps of snow to eastern Colorado. These storms come from the south and get moisture from the Gulf of Mexico. The moist air travels north to the east side of the Rocky Mountains. With these storms, eastern Colorado and the Front Range get heavy snow, but the Colorado mountains usually do not. After dumping snow in Colorado, these storms move east across the country.

That's One Snowy City!

During and after a giant snowstorm or blizzard, many things that usually go on in a city like Denver may be stopped for days. School is cancelled. Buses and cars can't get through the streets. Many stores are closed. Sometimes the power goes out. People snowshoe and ski through the streets and parks, build snowmen, and have snowball fights. Will a giant snowstorm or blizzard happen this winter? Perhaps! Take a look at the ruler to find out just how many inches of snow fell during some of Denver's most memorable snowstorms and blizzards.

DENVER'S BIGGEST SNOWSTORMS

← **46"** Dec. 1913

← **32"** Mar. 2003
← **30"** Nov. 1946

← **24"** Dec. 1982
← **22"** Nov. 1983
← **21"** Nov. 1991
← **19"** Mar. 1983
← **18"** Nov. 1978
← **17"** Mar. 1952 & April 1957
   16" Oct. 1969 & April 1972

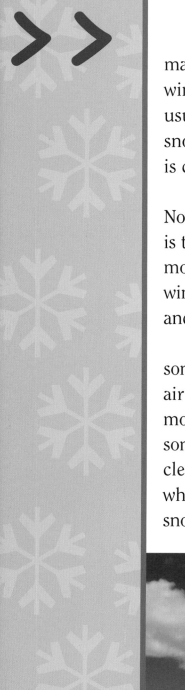

Thick Snows Cover the Mountains

Usually snow melts from the High Plains and from many places in the foothills in the days or weeks after a winter storm. High in Colorado's mountains, though, snow usually doesn't melt for months. Several hundred inches of snow can build up during the winter. This buildup of snow is called the *snowpack*.

Most snow falls on Colorado's Rocky Mountains between November and May. The snowiest place in the mountains is the Park Range, east of Steamboat Springs. These mountains get more snow than the others because the winter air moving over the Park Range is especially moist and perfect for making snow.

The San Juan Mountains in south-central Colorado sometimes get tons of snow, too. This happens when moist air from the West Coast makes its way to Colorado. This moist air usually flows over other mountains and loses some of its moisture along the way. But when it has steered clear of other mountains, the air is still full of moisture when it gets to the San Juan Mountains and dumps thick snow onto places like Wolf Creek Pass. There was a total of

A huge snowstorm brought several feet of fresh snow to Rabbit Ears Pass near Steamboat Springs.

838 inches of snow on Wolf Creek Pass during the winter of 1978–1979. That's almost 70 feet of snow, more than enough to cover a 6-story building!

Be Prepared for Snow Days!

Check the weather forecasts for Winter Storm Warnings, Heavy Snow Warnings, or Blizzard Warnings. If a big winter storm is headed your way, then it is time to prepare! You and your family might be stuck in the house for a few days if the snowstorm or blizzard is a big one, so make sure you have extra food and water. Sometimes heavy snow brings the electric power lines down. Make sure you have flashlights and batteries in case the electricity goes out in your home. And, of course, having a shovel or two to clear the snow is essential.

A Denver street after the 2003 blizzard

It is dangerous to drive as heavy snow is falling and blowing. If you must travel by car or truck, make sure to bring tire chains, a shovel, blankets, food, water, and a phone with you. Stay inside until the snow stops falling if you can.

Snowstorms and blizzards can be lots of fun once the snow has stopped. Playing in the snow is the best part! After the snow has stopped falling, wear your warm and waterproof winter clothes when you head outside to play. And don't forget mittens or gloves and a hat!

Denverites venture out after the 2003 blizzard.

There are as many as 20,000 avalanches in Colorado's mountains each year. An avalanche happens when snow moves quickly downhill. Some avalanches are loose, powdery snow moving downhill at speeds up to 30 mph. Others are gigantic slabs of snow that cover an entire mountainside and move at speeds up to 100 mph. All avalanches are dangerous, but gigantic slab avalanches are extremely dangerous. Even though avalanches are common, they only happen under special conditions. Read on to learn more about the special conditions that cause avalanches in Colorado.

Left: February 28, 1987, avalanche at Red Mountain Pass, Colorado.
Right: This avalanche happened on May 1, 2005, on a slope above Loveland Valley ski area, which had closed for the season. During the avalanche, a 3-foot thickness of snow, 200 feet across, slid about 250 vertical feet.

Unstable Snow

To make an avalanche, there needs to be snow! Snow builds up layer by layer with each new snowstorm or blizzard. After a big storm has left a layer of snow, the ice crystals that make up the snowflakes might grow together, making a strong layer of snow. But sometimes the ice crystals do not grow together. Over time, they become grainy like sugar. Slab avalanches happen when a strong layer lies above a weakly attached layer of grainy sugar snow. The strong layer slides down the slope on the weak layer just like a person slipping on a banana peel.

WEAK LAYER

STRONG LAYER

25-degree angle

50-degree angle

Steep Slopes

Just as a skateboard won't roll in a flat place on its own, snow won't slide if the land is not steep enough. The steepness, or slope, of mountainsides is measured in degrees. Flat land has a slope of 0 degrees. A cliff that goes straight up and down has a slope of 90 degrees. Most avalanches happen on mountainsides with slopes somewhere in the middle, from 25 to 50 degrees. If the slope is steeper than that, snow doesn't collect on it as much. If the slope is less steep, the snow is likely to stay put. Boulders, trees, and other things on the slope can also anchor the snow in place, preventing avalanches.

What Starts an Avalanche?

Avalanches can be started by loud noises like shouts or gunfire. Skiers, snowboarders, and snowmobiles traveling across unstable snow can also start avalanches. Trained professionals set off explosives to start avalanches on purpose. This gets unstable snow off mountainsides above towns, highways, and ski areas without hurting people. Most avalanches happen naturally without any help from people. However, most avalanches that trap people are started by the people who get trapped.

Left: A large avalanche knocks down the trees in its path, leaving a feature called a "chute." These chutes are near Silverton, Colorado, in the San Juan Mountains.
Right: An avalanche chute in the summertime in Colorado's San Juan Mountains.

Avalanche Safety

In Colorado, about 60 people are caught in avalanches each year. About six of those people die. The snow moves so quickly that people cannot run or ski out of its way. It is so powerful that it uproots trees on its way down the slope. People who have survived avalanches say that it feels like being trapped in concrete. The snow might have felt loose and fluffy at the surface, but it packs very tightly together after traveling down the mountain. A person trapped in the snow cannot move and will eventually run out of air if he or she is not dug out. Experts agree that the best way to survive an avalanche is to avoid being in one!

How do you avoid getting caught in an avalanche? Use your head and avoid places where avalanche danger is high. Ski

The blue areas show where most avalanches occur in Colorado.

areas keep avalanche danger low by blasting unstable snow. Flatter valleys are also safer. Never go out into the mountains in the winter without an adult who knows how to avoid avalanche danger. Also, be sure to visit the Colorado Avalanche Information Center website (http://geosurvey.state.co.us/avalanche/) for current avalanche conditions before you go.

Earthquakes move the ground with great shivers. Deep within the earth, rocks slide past each other, making a low rumbling noise. People caught in an earthquake can hear buildings rattle and glass break.

Not all earthquakes are the same. Some are very large and some are very small. The size of earthquakes, or the amount of energy they release, is often measured with the *Richter scale*. A small earthquake will have a number closer to 0 on the scale and a huge earthquake will have a number closer to 10.

The rocks on the outer part of the Earth are called *lithosphere*. This thick layer of hard, solid rock has sediments, soils, plants, water, and animals on its top surface. The lithosphere is broken into huge pieces called *plates* that fit

together like a puzzle. Below the rocky lithosphere is a layer of rock that is not as rigid. The lithosphere plates slide on the less rigid layer.

The largest earthquakes happen in places where the plates meet and bump against each other as they slide around. Colorado is not one of these places. The closest place where plates meet each other is California, where there are some very strong earthquakes. But Colorado still gets earthquakes, both along smaller breaks in rock, called *faults*, and from people making changes to the rock deep underground.

Sangre de Cristo Fault

In Colorado, the Sangre de Cristo Fault separates the Sangre de Cristo Mountains from the flat San Luis Valley.

Are There Really Earthquakes Here?

Earthquakes happen naturally in Colorado as rocks bump against each other along underground breaks called faults. Scientists make maps to show where faults are located so that people know about the hazard. However, people are the cause of many of the earthquakes that have happened in Colorado in the past 100 years. Mine blasts and underground

nuclear blasts have caused medium-size earthquakes. But most of the earthquakes made by people in Colorado happened when liquid was pumped deep underground. In the 1950s, water from sewers was pumped 2 miles deep into the earth at the Rocky Mountain Arsenal near Denver. Less than a year after workers started pumping the water, thousands of small earthquakes and a couple of larger ones happened in the area. At the time, nobody knew that pumping the water into the ground could cause earthquakes.

Since 1995, salty water has been pumped underground in southwest Colorado's Paradox Valley so that the salt does not get into the Dolores and Colorado Rivers. This has kept the rivers free of salt, but it has also caused more than 3,000 minor earthquakes. Most of these little quakes are so small that people do not feel them.

How Often Are There Earthquakes?

Earthquakes are not considered a huge threat in Colorado. People are not too concerned about them and it is pretty rare that there is even a medium-size one. However, they do happen! Since 1867, there have been

Colorado's largest recorded earthquakes and the years they happened.

nearly 500 earthquakes in Colorado that are a magnitude of 2.5 or greater on the Richter scale. That might seem like a lot of shaking, but for comparison, over the same time there have been more than 20,000 earthquakes of similar size in California! Colorado has more earthquake danger than the states to the east, like Oklahoma and Kansas, but much less earthquake danger than Nevada and California.

The largest earthquake ever recorded in Colorado happened on November 7, 1882. The center of the earthquake was 10 miles north of the mountain town of Estes Park. It shook Denver and the Front Range with a magnitude of 6.6 on the Richter scale, which is pretty unusual for this state. In fact, it is pretty unusual altogether. Only 14 out of the 50 states in the country have experienced an earthquake that strong. In 135 years, there have been 15 somewhat similar or slightly smaller earthquakes in Colorado. During earthquakes like these, people have trouble walking, objects fly off shelves, pictures fall from walls, and furniture dances around the room. By studying rocks and layers of earth, we know that even stronger earthquakes happened when Native Americans were the only inhabitants of Colorado. Scientists say that Colorado has low to moderate earthquake danger. That means that strong earthquakes happen only very rarely, but they can happen again!

What to Do if There Is an Earthquake

During an earthquake, stay clear of falling objects. Remember not to stand under bookshelves or anything large and heavy. Standing in a doorway is one of the safest places to be during an earthquake. Luckily, your chances of being in a big earthquake in Colorado are pretty low compared to the states to our west!

Have you ever heard the saying, "What goes up, must come down?" Well, millions of years ago, Colorado's Rocky Mountains were pushed up and ever since then they have been coming down, bit by bit. Rocks fall off and roll downhill. Some are the size of baseballs and others are the size of houses. Occasionally, landslides happen and an entire slope moves downhill, including all the boulders, pebbles, and soil on it. Mudslides also happen in Colorado when water mixes with mud and flows downhill.

Watch Out for Falling Rocks!

Rockfalls happen mostly in the mountains, where rocks on steep mountain slopes sometimes become unstable and tumble downward. There are many reasons why rocks can become unstable. For example, rain and melting snow in the early spring can cause water to seep into cracks in the

Left: This mudslide dumped tons of mud onto Interstate 70 near Glenwood Springs, Colorado. **Center:** These rocks fell onto Interstate 70 near El Rancho. The largest boulders that fell during this rockfall weighed more than 200 tons! **Right:** This landslide near McClure Pass, south of Aspen, damaged the road. A car drove into the hole where the road used to be. Luckily, no one was hurt.

This mudflow happened near Arapahoe Basin ski area in 1999.

rock. The water freezes and thaws over and over again as temperatures change. Water freezing in a crack in the rock expands, breaking the rock apart. Rocks can also be broken apart when tree roots grow through them.

It's a Landslide!

While a rockfall is just one or a few falling rocks, a landslide is a whole hillside of rocks and soil moving downhill. Landslides are common in Colorado and happen when the rocks or plant roots holding the slope in place give way. Some landslides move very quickly, more than 10 feet per second. Others move very slowly, less than an inch per year. Landslides cause more than $3,000,000 in damage to buildings in Colorado each year.

A huge landslide can bury a house or even an entire village. More than 100 years ago in the mountains west of

The red places on the map show where landslides are most likely.

Denver, there was a small mining town called Brownsville just west of the town of Silver Plume. Heavy rain triggered a tremendous landslide that covered the entire town. The town is now underground under Interstate 70.

People sometimes accidentally trigger landslides by digging on a steep hillside, adding material to the top of a hill, or adding moisture to the land. But landslides are often completely natural events.

Mudslides Go With the Flow

A mudslide is fast-moving water, sand, and mud mixed together. It is thick like a milkshake, but not as tasty! Mud might not seem very powerful, but when it is moving quickly during a mudslide, it can sweep buildings, trees, cars, and boulders away.

Like flash floods, mudslides can happen without much warning after a quick thunderstorm or snowmelt, usually during the spring and summer. Mudslides happen mainly in steep areas in the mountains, especially places where there are very few plants covering the soil.

For More Information

Weather Events
(including thunderstorms, tornadoes, wind, and snow)

- National Center for Atmospheric Research, Boulder, Colorado, offers exhibits and tours of its Mesa Lab (http://eo.ucar.edu/visit/).

- NCAR Kids' Crossing is a website where kids can learn about weather and climate through stories, articles, and activities (http://eo.ucar.edu/kids/).

- The National Weather Service gives the latest weather forecasts and information about hazards, warnings, and conditions.
   Denver/Boulder
   (http://www.crh.noaa.gov/den/)
   Grand Junction
   (http://www.crh.noaa.gov/gjt/)
   Pueblo
   (http://www.crh.noaa.gov/pub/)

- Community Collaborative Rain, Hail, and Snow Network (CoCoRaHS) volunteers track local precipitation (http://www.cocorahs.org/).

- NOAA Playtime for Kids is a website with information and activities about weather events (http://www.nws.noaa.gov/om/reachout/kidspage.shtml).

Flash Floods

- Flood safety information from FEMA for Kids (http://www.fema.gov/kids/floods.htm)

- "Wild Ride During a Flash Flood," a story for kids about what it is like to be in a flash flood (http://eo.ucar.edu/kids/dangerwx/tstorm8.htm)

Wildfires

- Colorado State Forest Service (http://www.colostate.edu/Depts/CSFS/fireinfo.html)

High Altitudes

- NOVA Online Adventure: Everest by PBS explains what the altitude is like on the world's highest mountain (http://www.pbs.org/wgbh/nova/everest/exposure/).

- Colorado Mountain Club Youth Education Program has a variety of classes for groups, including Physiology with Altitude, about the effects of high altitude (http://www.cmc.org).

- *What's Up with Altitude: Mr. Moffat's Class Investigates How Altitude Affects Our Bodies* is a book with stories and crafts to explore our atmosphere, altitude, and altitude sickness. (http://www.cmc.org/).

Avalanches

- Colorado Avalanche Information Center (http://geosurvey.state.co.us/avalanche/)

- Avalanche Science class at the Colorado Mountain Club Youth Education Program (http://www.cmc.org/)

Earthquakes, Rockfalls, and Landslides

- Colorado Geological Survey (http://geosurvey.state.co.us/)

- The U.S. Geological Survey Learning Web (http://education.usgs.gov/)